California's

Indian Nations

Ben Nussbaum

Consultants

Kristina Jovin, M.A.T.
Alvord Unified School District
Teacher of the Year

Vanessa Ann Gunther, Ph.D.
Department of History
Chapman University

Publishing Credits

Rachelle Cracchiolo, M.S.Ed., *Publisher*
Conni Medina, M.A.Ed., *Managing Editor*
Emily R. Smith, M.A.Ed., *Series Developer*
June Kikuchi, *Content Director*
Marc Pioch, M.A.Ed., and Susan Daddis, M.A.Ed., *Editors*
Courtney Roberson, *Senior Graphic Designer*

Image Credits: Cover and p.1 J. T. Vintage/Bridgeman Images; pp.2–3 Museum of Fine Arts, Houston, Texas, USA/Bridgeman Images; pp.4–5 Butte County Historical Society; p.5 (top) Courtesy of the Phoebe A. Hearst Museum of Anthropology and the Regents of the University of California, Photography by Alfred L. Kroeber, (Catalog No. 15-5698); pp.6 (bottom), back cover Pomo basket with shell beads, Pomo Indians, Creator, ©Photo courtesy of the Fowler Museum at UCLA, Photograph by Don Cole; p.7 Mark Hallett Paleoart/Science Source; p.8 Bateau du port de San Francisco [ca. 1815], Voyage pittoresque autour du monde : avec des portraits de sauvages d'Amerique, d'Asie, d'Afrique, et des iles du Grand ocean : des paysages, des vues maritimes, et plusieurs objets d'histoire naturelle : accompagne de descriptions par m. le baron Cuvier, fG420.K84C6.1822 -- Part 3, Plate X. Courtesy of The Bancroft Library, University of California, Berkeley; p.10 Mrs. James V. Rosemeyre; Bakersfield; July 1905, C. Hart Merriam collection of Native American photographs [graphic], BANC PIC 1978.008 Y/24NP2 no.1--PIC. Courtesy of The Bancroft Library, University of California, Berkeley; p.12 (bottom) Photo by Daniel Medina; pp.12–13 Attributed to Ferdinand Deppe, San Gabriel Mission, Oil on canvas, c.1832. 27 x 37 inches, Gift of Nancy Dustin Wall Moure. 1994.083. Laguna Art Museum; p.14 (pipe) Gabrielino steatite pipe, Gabrielino Indians, Creator, ©Photo courtesy of the Fowler Museum at UCLA, Photograph by Don Cole; p.17 (upper right) David Rumsey Map Collection, www.davidrumsey.com; p.18 Houses and House-Life of the American Aborigines by Lewis H. Morgan, Department of the Interior, U.S. Geographical and Geological Survey of the Rocky Mountain Region; p.19 (full page) Bobbi Onia/Underwood Archives/Getty Images, (upper right) Library of Congress [LC-USZ62-118769]; p.20 U.S. National Archives and Records Administration; p.21 Everett Collection Inc/Alamy Stock Photo; p.24 Illustration by J.R. Browne in Crusoe's Island: A Ramble in the Footsteps of Alexander Selkirk with Sketches of Adventure in California and Washoe by J. Ross Browne; p.25 Courtesy of the Phoebe A. Hearst Museum of Anthropology and the Regents of the University of California, Photography by Alfred L. Kroeber, (Catalog No. 15-5797); p.26 Alfred and Theodora Kroeber sitting on steps of cabin, circa 1927, AL. Kroeber family photographs [graphic], BANC PIC 1978.128--PIC, Box 1. Courtesy of The Bancroft Library, University of California, Berkeley; p.27 Courtesy of the Phoebe A. Hearst Museum of Anthropology and the Regents of the University of California, Photography by Alfred L. Kroeber, (Catalog No. 15-5435); p.29 Granger, NYC; p.32 Courtesy of the Phoebe A. Hearst Museum of Anthropology and the Regents of the University of California, Photography by Alfred L. Kroeber, (Catalog No. 15-5698); all other images from iStock and/or Shutterstock.

Library of Congress Cataloging-in-Publication Data
Names: Nussbaum, Ben, 1975- author.
Title: California's Indian nations / Ben Nussbaum.
Description: Huntington Beach, CA : Teacher Created Materials, [2017] | Includes index. | Audience: Grades 4-6.
Identifiers: LCCN 2017014089 (print) | LCCN 2017014329 (ebook) | ISBN 9781425835026 (eBook) | ISBN 9781425832322 (pbk.)
Subjects: LCSH: Indians of North America--California--Juvenile literature. | Gabrielino Indians--Juvenile literature. | Yokuts Indians--Juvenile literature. | CYAC: Yana Indians--Juvenile literature.
Classification: LCC E78.C15 (ebook) | LCC E78.C15 N87 2017 (print) | DDC 979.4/00497--dc23
LC record available at https://lccn.loc.gov/2017014089

Teacher Created Materials
5301 Oceanus Drive
Huntington Beach, CA 92649-1030
http://www.tcmpub.com

ISBN 978-1-4258-3232-2

Printed in China
Nordica.012019.CA21801581

Table of Contents

The Lone Survivor

In 1911, California was developing into a modern state. Cars were replacing horses. Telephones and electricity were making their ways into homes.

In the city of Oroville, California, the local sheriff received a call. A starving man had been caught stealing meat. The man did not speak a language that anyone was familiar with. He had leather strips through holes in his ears. A piece of wood pierced his nose. He wore a **loincloth** made of bearskin.

Newspapers spread the story of this strange person. Eventually, scholars discovered that he spoke the language of the Yahi. The Yahi were part of the Yana tribe. No one else in town spoke the language.

Tribes Today

Today, there are many active native tribes around the world. They continue to fight for equal rights. Not all of these tribes have been able to protect their **ancestral** lands. Still, they remain true to their cultures and ways of life.

Civics

Oroville, California

In fact, no one else from his tribe could be found alive.

This man, Ishi, became famous. Reporters called him the last "untamed" American Indian. He had spent his whole life in the hills, living the same way his ancestors had for thousands of years. Now, he found himself in a modern society. In some ways, Ishi was the last chapter in a meaningful book about the Yana.

Ishi demonstrates how to use a bow and arrow

A Lost Name

In Yahi culture, people did not speak their own names. Even though he was the last of his tribe, Ishi followed this **taboo**. People called him "Ishi" because it means "man" in the Yahi language.

Change in a Golden Land

About 14,000 years ago, humans first set foot in what is now California. It was a much different place then!

Woolly mammoths and mastodons, both elephant-like animals, moved in herds across the land. Giant sloths picked leaves off trees. Camels munched on grass.

People hunted and ate these beasts. But soon, some of these huge animals became **extinct**. The first Californians had to find new ways to survive. Tribes moved to new places searching for food. They spread their cultures as they went.

Luckily, these cultures are not lost. Before the Spanish arrived, American Indians did not read or write. So, there are no written records from the early tribes. But, historians have studied **artifacts**. These **primary sources** give clues about out how the tribes lived.

Animal bones show what they ate. Burial sites share information about their beliefs. Baskets offer a look into their daily lives. All these items tell about these people of the past.

Tightly woven baskets like this could carry water.

Fierce Competition

Huge animals served as food sources for early tribes. But these animals were also food for other predators, such as saber-toothed cats and dire wolves. Early tribes had to defeat not just their prey, but other predators, too.

High-Tech Hunt

California Indians used several weapons to hunt. A common weapon was the *atlatl* (AHT-lah-tuhl). This device helped to hurl spears. The atlatl was a very advanced weapon. It let humans hunt from far away instead of having to strike animals up close.

Bones from woolly mammoths and other animals have been found in tar pits in California.

Not all California Indians lived the same way. Picture a tribe that lived on flat land near the ocean. One day, some of its members moved into the hills. The plants and animals there were not the same as what they ate before. The air was cooler. The people in the hills had to learn new ways to live. They created new words to describe their lives.

Now, imagine that thousands of years have passed. The two groups have developed different customs. What started as one tribe turned into two separate tribes. That is how California Indians became so varied.

Spanish explorers came to the region in 1769. There were already about 300,000 California Indians living there. But they were not a single group. They formed many tribes. In some areas, four or five tribes lived within a day's walk of each other. In other areas, tribes could go years without seeing someone from another tribe. Each tribe had its own way of life. These differences made California very **diverse**!

American Indians in San Francisco's port, drawing, 1815

Say What?

Some historians think there were almost a hundred languages in California before settlers arrived. And there were many more **dialects**. There was such a wide range that members of the same tribe might have had a hard time speaking to each other!

Near the Ocean

No one knows what early California Indians in the Los Angeles area called themselves. Most experts think it was *Tongva* (TON-vah). Some think it was *Kizh* (KIHZ).

The Tongva Indians were masters of the ocean. Canoes were central to their lives. Today, historians study Tongva canoes to learn more about the tribe. All Tongva canoes were built the same way. In the first step, they selected driftwood logs and let them dry. Next, the Tongva formed planks. They used antlers or whalebones to cut the wood. They connected the planks with rope. Then, the Tongva coated the canoe to make it waterproof.

Because the Tongva relied so heavily on the sea, they stayed near the ocean. Most of the tribe lived in present-day Los Angeles. Some traveled to the Channel Islands off the coast of Southern California.

Narcisa Higuera was one of the last Tongva speakers. She provided a lot of information about her tribe's culture.

Fox Forward

Foxes live on six of the eight Channel Islands (shown below). Historians think American Indian tribes brought foxes to the southern islands thousands of years ago. The tribes may have brought foxes for their fur. Other tribes may have kept them as pets.

Geography

Resources

The Tongva tribe used a tar-like substance called *asphaltum* on their canoes. It acts like glue and makes things waterproof. Asphaltum is still around. It is the tar that washes up on beaches. Though it may be a bother now, hundreds of years ago, it carried value for the Tongva tribe.

Geography

In 1771, Spanish priests began calling local tribes *Gabrieliños* (GAH-bree-eh-lee-nyos). In that year, they built a mission in Los Angeles. They named it *Mission San Gabriel Arcángel*. Priests hoped to use the mission to **convert** nearby American Indians. One of those tribes was the Tongva. The priests hoped to change the Tongva's way of life. They made the Tongva work on the mission's farms. They also fed Spanish foods to the Tongva. The priests thought those were good ways to make the tribes follow Spanish customs.

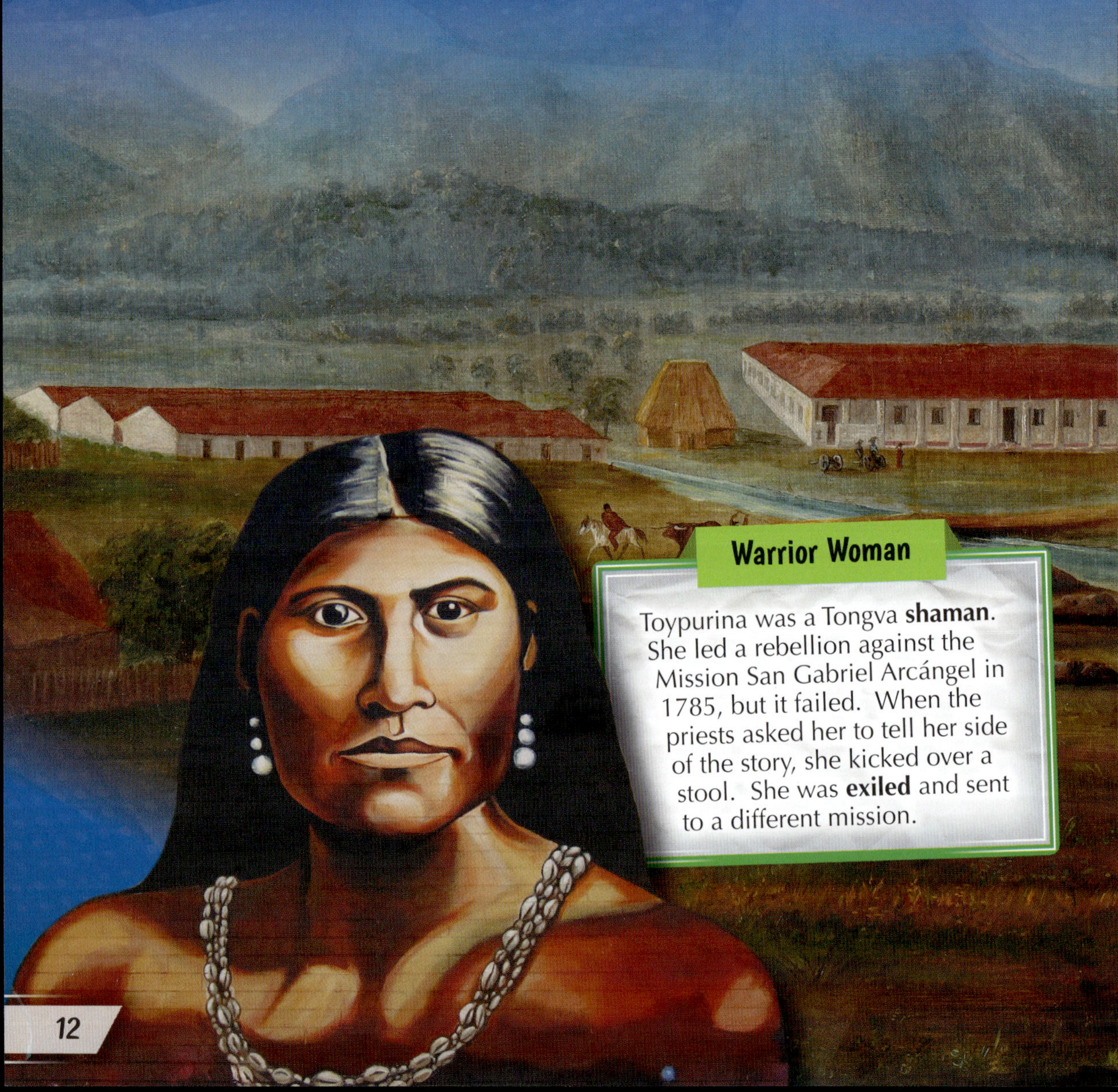

Warrior Woman

Toypurina was a Tongva **shaman**. She led a rebellion against the Mission San Gabriel Arcángel in 1785, but it failed. When the priests asked her to tell her side of the story, she kicked over a stool. She was **exiled** and sent to a different mission.

Some Tongva members stayed at the mission. Others tried to flee. But, Spanish soldiers forced them back. They whipped the Tongva to show the rest of the tribe what would happen if they tried to leave, too. While at the missions, the Tongva were exposed to new diseases, which killed many of them. There were about 5,000 Tongva when the mission was built. Within a few decades, that number **plummeted**.

Caring for Livestock

The Mission San Gabriel Arcángel had huge herds of animals. At its peak, there were 25,000 cattle and almost as many sheep. The Tongva tribe and other natives had to keep all those animals healthy!

Economics

Mission San Gabriel Arcángel

Before the Spanish arrived, the Tongva traded shells and fish. They also traded soapstone. This is a soft stone that can be carved into bowls and pots. They thrived. After life at the mission, the Tongva tribe changed. Many members had died or run away. Others had converted to Christianity. They did not wish to remain part of the traditional tribe anymore. As a result, the Tongva customs were almost lost to history.

Today, the remaining Tongva are trying to rebuild the tribe. Different groups want to lead the Tongva. Each group's members think they know what is best for the future of the tribe. But they are having a hard time agreeing with each other.

The Tongva are recognized as a tribe by California but not by the U.S. government. There is a lot of work to do to change this. If they are recognized, the Tongva will receive valuable benefits. They will be stronger. They might flourish once again. Until then, the Tongva tribe must continue working to keep their culture alive.

Tongva soapstone pipe

Dangerous Tea

The Tongva had a religious ritual that spread throughout the area. It involved drinking tea made from poisonous Jimsonweed. If the tea was too powerful, it could kill a person!

Jimsonweed

Today, Mission San Gabriel Arcángel is used as a church and school.

Listen Up!

Pamela Munro is a professor at the University of California, Los Angeles. She helped the Tongva people. She posted recordings of herself speaking their language. You can go online and hear Tongva!

In the Valley

Like the Los Angeles basin, California's Central Valley is **fertile** and flat. Today, the valley is mostly farmland. Fields stretch as far as the eye can see. But hundreds of years ago, it was a wild place. Rivers and streams jumped with fish. Clams crowded the bottoms of lakes. Deer, elk, and antelope lived on the edges of huge swamps.

The Yokuts tribe lived on this wild land. Historians believe that there were between 50,000 and 70,000 Yokuts. The Yokuts were actually a group of up to 50 smaller tribes. *Yokuts* means "people." The name is fitting for the number of people it represented.

The Spanish called the Yokuts *Tulareños* (too-lahr-EH-nyos) after the **tules** (TOO-lees) that filled the valley. These plants played a huge role in the lives of the Yokuts.

Tule Elk

Historians believe California may have been home to up to half a million tule elk in the late 1700s. A century later, there were only a few left. Many people tried to save the tule elk from extinction. Their hard work paid off. There are now tule elk herds in many California state parks.

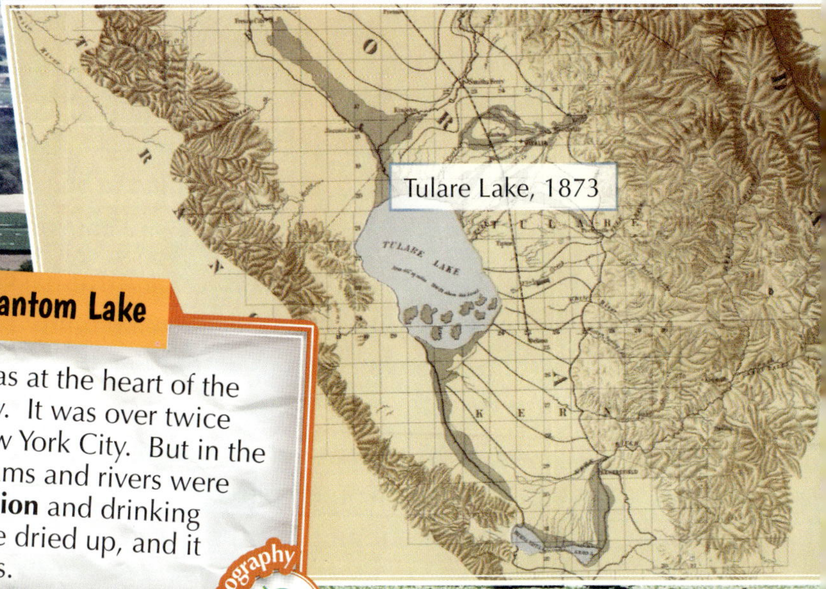

Tulare Lake, 1873

Phantom Lake

Tulare Lake was at the heart of the Yokuts territory. It was over twice the size of New York City. But in the 1930s, its streams and rivers were used for **irrigation** and drinking water. The lake dried up, and it no longer exists.

Geography

A herd of tule elk grazes in a valley.

The Yokuts ate the roots of tules. They used tules to make clothes and create walls for their homes. They built rafts and canoes out of tules, tying together bundles of the **buoyant** reed. The canoes did not last long, but they were easy to make.

The Yokuts were famous for their beautiful baskets. They used tules and other materials to make many types of baskets. One type was used to gather berries. Another might be used for collecting acorns. One was used specifically for **winnowing**. A tray-like basket was used for a game that Yokuts women played. Some Yokuts baskets were waterproof and could be used to make soup. The Yokuts even pushed children across rivers by placing them in large baskets.

tule lodges in 1877

Costly Baskets

If you want to buy antique Yokuts baskets today, you will need to start saving your money. They typically cost thousands of dollars.

Economics

This photograph shows two California Indians on a tule canoe.

Do-It-Yourself

Do you feel like making a boat? There are many classes in California that teach people how to make canoes from tules. If enough people help, a canoe can be made in just a few hours.

Like the Tongva tribe to the south, many Yokuts also lived in missions. Some Yokuts fled. Others wanted to fight. One Yokuts man led the most successful **revolt**. His name was Estanislao (es-THAN-ih-SLOW).

Estanislao fled Mission San Jose around 1828. Later that year, he returned with hundreds of local native people. They hid in the thick brush and attacked Spanish soldiers. As news of his triumph spread, more native people joined him. Within a few months, he had almost a thousand people on his side. Estanislao was never captured. After a year of fighting Spanish soldiers, he took refuge in a different mission. A priest forgave him and let him stay.

This letter reveals that the U.S. Senate secretly rejected the treaties.

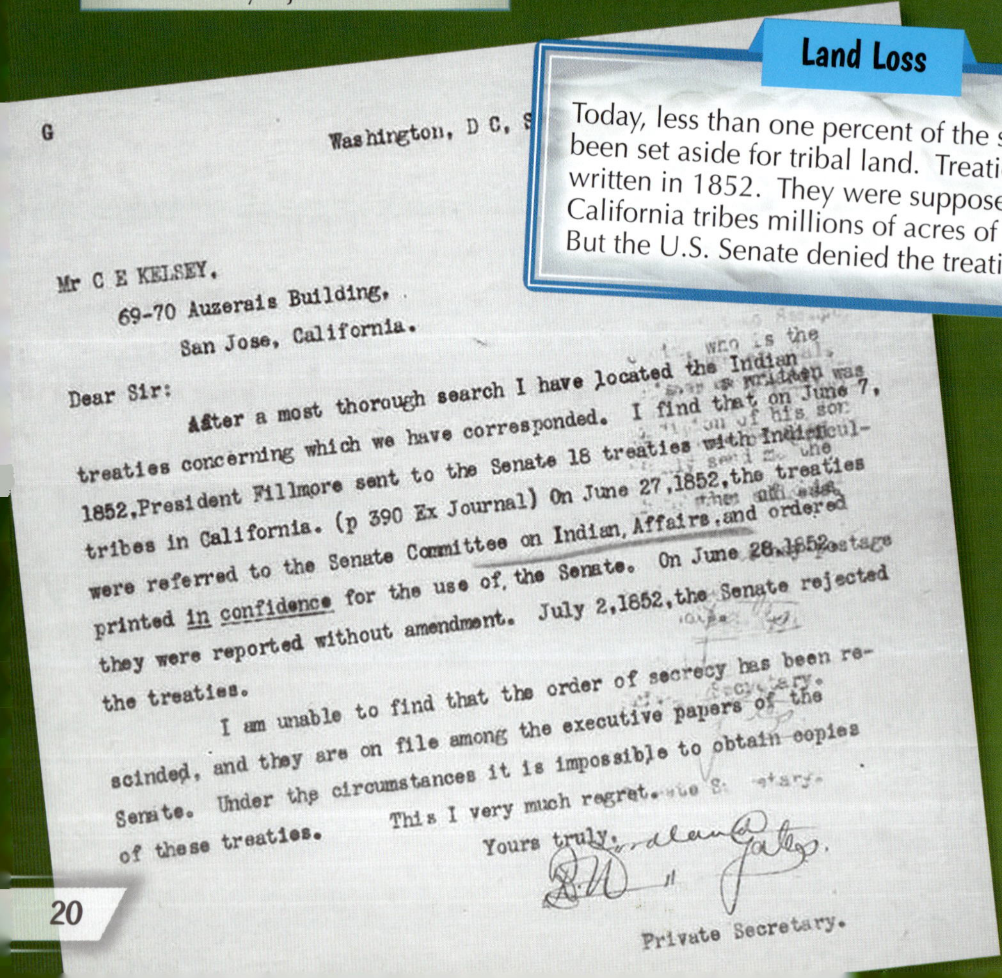

G

Washington, D C,

Mr C E KELSEY,
69-70 Auzerais Building,
San Jose, California.

Dear Sir:

After a most thorough search I have located the Indian treaties concerning which we have corresponded. I find that on June 7, 1852, President Fillmore sent to the Senate 18 treaties with Indian tribes in California. (p 390 Ex Journal) On June 27,1852, the treaties were referred to the Senate Committee on Indian Affairs, and ordered printed <u>in confidence</u> for the use of the Senate. On June 28,1852 they were reported without amendment. July 2,1852, the Senate rejected the treaties.

I am unable to find that the order of secrecy has been rescinded, and they are on file among the executive papers of the Senate. Under the circumstances it is impossible to obtain copies of these treaties. This I very much regret.

Yours truly,

Private Secretary.

Land Loss

Today, less than one percent of the state has been set aside for tribal land. Treaties were written in 1852. They were supposed to give California tribes millions of acres of land. But the U.S. Senate denied the treaties.

Civics

The Yokuts fought the Spanish, but they could not fight disease. Illnesses killed many Yokuts. Gold miners also caused problems for the tribe. The mining process **polluted** swamps and lakes. The few Yokuts who were left struggled to survive.

In recent years, the Yokuts have grown stronger. Today, there are about 4,000 Yokuts in the state. They are building a new role for their tribe in the valley that has been their home for thousands of years.

Honoring a Rebel

Estanislao was a leader of the Yokuts. Stanislaus County was named after him. The county is in the heart of Yokuts land. The Stanislaus River was also named after him. It flows from the mountains to the San Joaquin River.

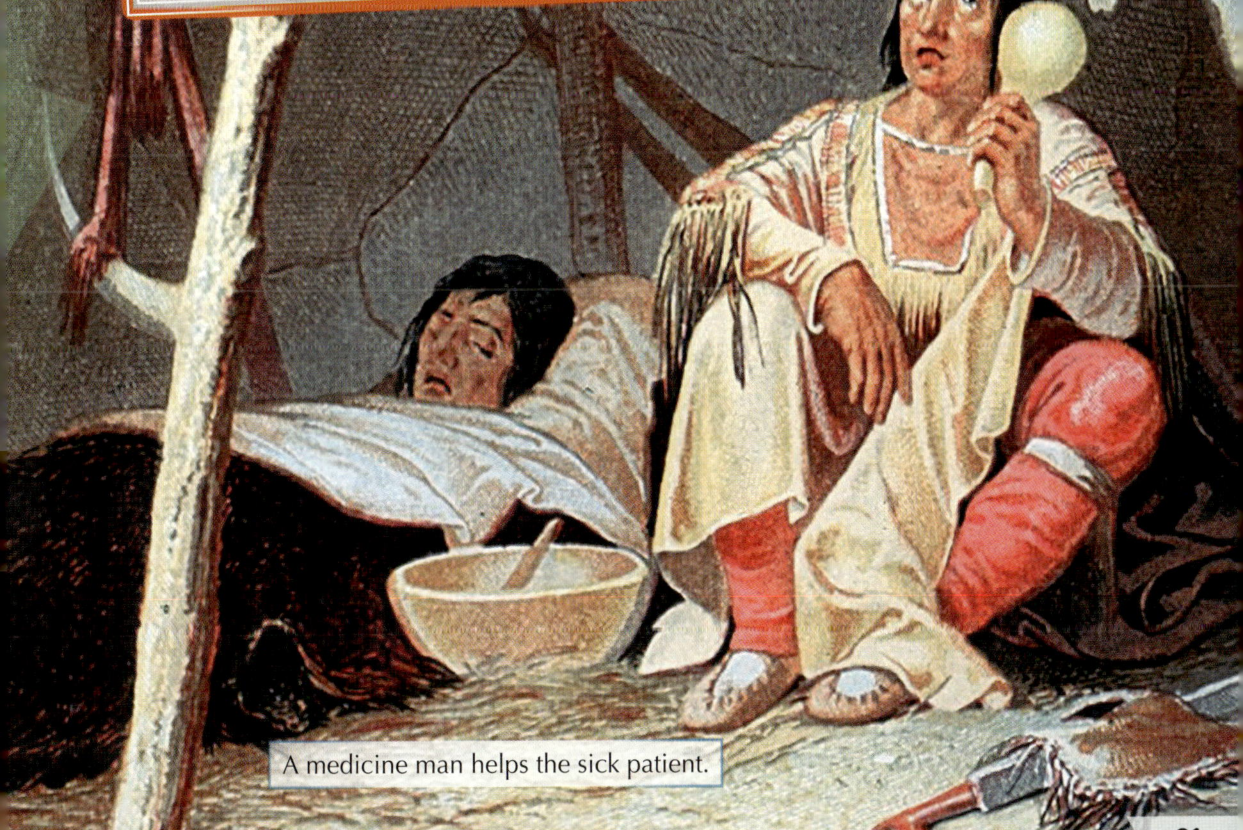

A medicine man helps the sick patient.

Rough Country

North of the Tongva and Yokuts tribes lived the Yana tribe. They called the land around Mount Lassen in Northern California home. The region is full of deep valleys and steep **gorges**.

Life in the mountains can be hard. With few resources, the Yana depended on two types of nuts to survive: acorns and buckeyes. In most years, acorns were easily gathered. They provided healthy and filling meals. And best of all, they could be stored for food during the winter months.

The Yana also relied on buckeye nuts. These nuts can be poisonous. The Yana put the poison from buckeye nuts into small pools of water. Any fish in the water would be stunned, making them easy to gather. The Yana tribe could live off fish and acorns all year.

Mount Lassen

These grinding holes were used to grind acorns into flour.

Preparing Acorns

To eat acorns, the Yana separated the nuts from the shells. Then, they ground the nuts into powder. The powder was filtered to make it less bitter. Finally, the powder could be cooked and eaten. Preparing acorns was a very time-consuming process.

Acorn Jelly

Today, acorns are popular in many Asian countries. Acorn powder can be found at Asian grocery stores. The powder is used to make a dish called *acorn jelly*. Acorn jelly is popular in South. Korea.

For many years, no settlers bothered the Yana tribe. People close to the area did not value the Yana land because there were so many rocks. Then, the Gold Rush started. Settlers crowded onto Yana land hoping to strike it rich.

The Yana fought to defend their homes. They were a fierce people and were feared by many other tribes. But the settlers were **ruthless.** One day in 1867, settlers killed 33 Yana people. Bodies lay on the ground. There was not enough of the Yana tribe left to bury their dead.

A group of settlers attacks California Indians.

The land around Mount Lassen is rugged and rocky.

No Help for Native People

California's leaders mistreated native tribes. As more and more settlers came, nothing was done to keep tribes safe. There were no laws to punish people who killed native people.

In about 40 years, the number of Yana in the state went from nearly 2,000 to a few dozen. The last of the tribe hid in the hills for years. This includes Ishi, the California Indian found in Oroville in 1911. He lived through **massacres** (MAH-sih-kuhrs) when he was a boy. Ishi watched his friends and family members die over the years. The Yana tribe shrunk. In the end, it was just Ishi.

Unique Language

The Yana language was different from most other languages. Men and women used different words to say the same thing. For example, women said *ha* for water, and men said *hana*.

Ishi makes a bow.

Two Worlds

When Ishi came out of the hills, the world had changed. People treated him better than his tribe had been treated in the past. Ishi taught scholars about his tribe. He showed people how he hunted and how he made arrows. He shared his songs. People continue to study Ishi today.

Ishi's death in 1916 closed a chapter in the history of the state. There are no more Yana. Many other native groups are gone, too. Traditions have been lost to time.

However, new traditions are being formed. More than 600,000 California Indians live in the state now. No state has a higher native population. Their communities are growing stronger. They work to keep their cultures alive and their pasts remembered. They also work to be a huge part of the state's future.

Theodora and Alfred Kroeber

Tribal Information

Much of what people know about California Indians comes from the Kroeber family. They studied all the tribes. The Kroebers wrote many books about what they learned. Their most important book was published in 1925. It is the *Handbook of the Indians of California*. Though old, many scholars still use the book.

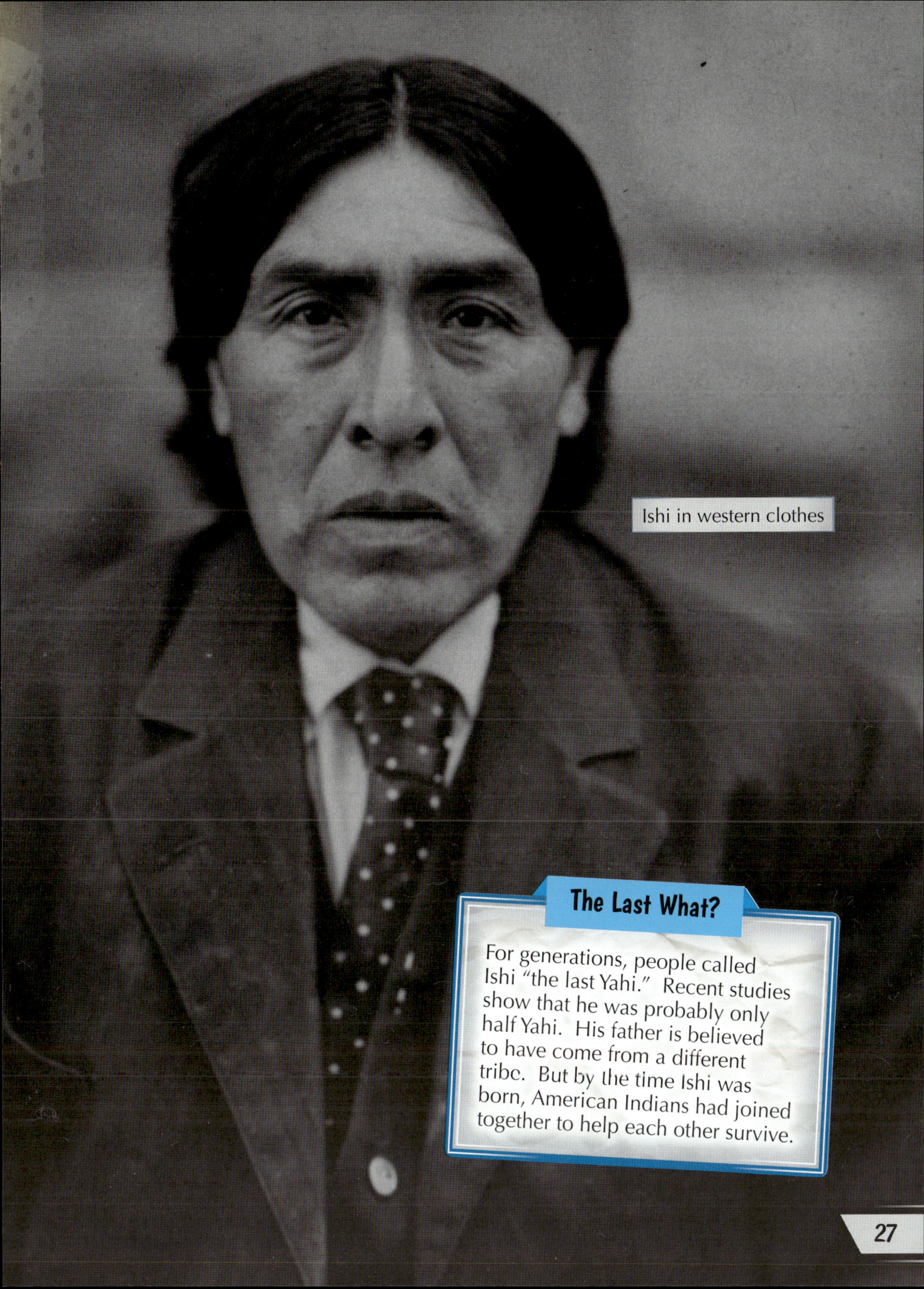

Ishi in western clothes

The Last What?

For generations, people called Ishi "the last Yahi." Recent studies show that he was probably only half Yahi. His father is believed to have come from a different tribe. But by the time Ishi was born, American Indians had joined together to help each other survive.

Explore It!

California Indians were great at using what they found in nature. Some tribes made fishhooks from shells. Other tribes made dice from walnuts. Some natives even made whistles from bird bones.

Step outside, and try to find something in nature that could help you survive. Is there a stick that can help you fish or plants you could turn into rope? What could you use to make art?

Find something you want to use, and then experiment with it. What happens if you soak it? What if you let it sit in the sun? How does it change? Show your finished product to friends and family members. Ask them for other ways to improve your creation. Then, apply their feedback. Did your changes make the product better or worse? Using these steps, create two things that would have helped you survive as a California Indian.

arrowhead spear

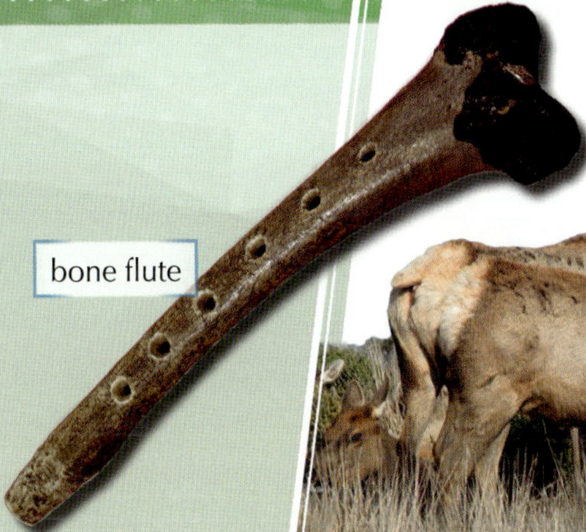

bone flute

shell dish

knife blade
with wood and
asphaltum handle

Glossary

ancestral—passed down from family

artifacts—simple objects that were made by humans in the past

buoyant—able to float

convert—to change from one religion or belief to another

dialects—different versions of one language that are spoken in particular areas

diverse—made up of things that are different from each other

exiled—forced out of one's country

extinct—no longer existing

fertile—capable of supporting the growth of many plants

gorges—deep, narrow places between mountains or hills

irrigation—the act of supplying lands with water by taking it from streams, rivers, or lakes

loincloth—a piece of cloth around the hips

massacres—the violent killings of many people

plummeted—went down sharply in number

polluted—land, water, or air that has been made dirty and not safe to use

primary sources—firsthand accounts of an event; documents or artifacts created during the time period being studied

revolt—an attempt to end someone's authority

ruthless—showing no pity or mercy

shaman—someone who is believed to be able to cure sick people

taboo—something that is forbidden by society

tules—tall reedlike plants that grow in marshy areas

winnowing—removing unwanted parts of a grain, seed, or nut

Index

Your Turn!

Read All About It

Imagine you are a reporter when the sheriff is called about Ishi. You've been assigned to cover his story. Write a newspaper article about how he was found. Interview the sheriff and other townspeople. Find out how he has been surviving on his own. What are the sheriff and townspeople going to do to help him? What will his future be? Be sure to include a headline.